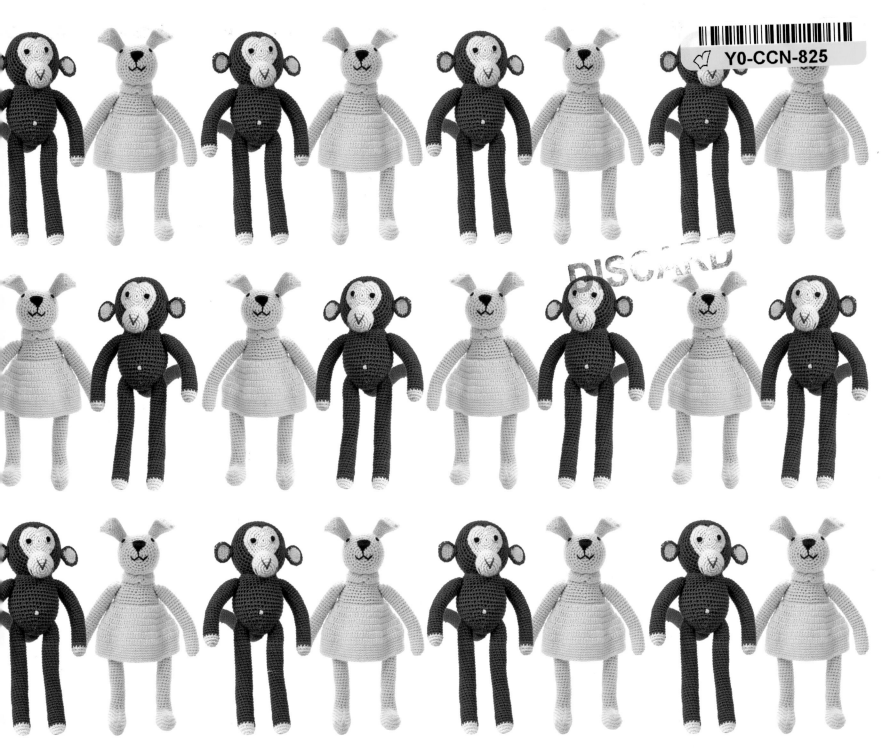

Título original: *Chimp & Bunny*
Copyright © 2017 Anne-Claire Petit
www.anneclarepetit.nl
Publicado por primera vez en 2017 por Rubinstein Publishing B.V., Amsterdam, the Netherlands

© Concepto y diseño original: Anne-Claire Petit
© Fotografía original: Jeroen Evers
© Diseño fotográfico original: Janneke van der Velden
© Diseño gráfico original: Mariëlle Tolenaar – studiosap

Agradecimientos especiales: Suzy Zeilmaker, Eléonore de Bruine y Linda van Velthoven

Publicado por Lata de Sal por acuerdo con Rubinstein Publishing B.V., Amsterdam, the Netherlands

© de esta edición: Lata de Sal, 2018

www.latadesal.com
info@latadesal.com

© de la traducción: Irene Álvarez Lata
© del diseño de la colección y la maquetación: Aresográfico
Impreso en Egedsa
ISBN: 978-84-949182-5-4 / Depósito legal: M-28966-2018
Impreso en España

Afortunadamente, un libro cosido con amor.

Este libro fue publicado con el apoyo de la Fundación neerlandesa de letras.

Nederlands
letterenfonds
dutch foundation
for literature

el maravilloso mundo
de **Chimp** y **Bunny**

anne-claire petit

LATAde**SAL**
Afortunada

the train station   la estación de tren

dog walker
paseador de perros

traveler
viajero

newspaper
periódico

stop sign
señal de alto

rope
cuerda

clock
reloj

platform **2** departure **11.15** **Paris**

display
letrero informativo

suitcase
maleta

train conductor
chofer de tren

the beach la playa

ball
pelota

sailboat
velero

lemonade
limonada

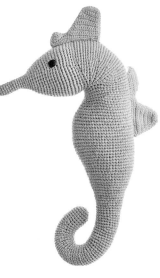

seahorse
caballito de mar

surfer
surfista

message in a bottle
mensaje en una botella

sardine
sardina

starfish
estrella de mar

bucket
cubeta

camera
cámara fotográfica

the film set el set de rodaje

actress
actriz

tape recorder
grabadora

visitor
visitante

plant
planta

megaphone
megáfono

clapperboard
claqueta

actor
actor

heart
corazón

film director
director de cine

the school la escuela

clock
reloj

ruler
regla

apple
manzana

pencils
lápices

satchel
mochila

teacher
profesor

paper airplane
avión de papel

books
libros

globe
globo terráqueo

student
estudiante

the shop la tienda

candy jar
tarro de dulces

lemon
limón

shopping bag
bolsa para
las compras

jam
mermelada

sausage
salchicha

shopkeeper
vendedor

shopping cart
carro de compras

scales
báscula

carrot
zanahoria

puppy
perro cachorro

the tennis court la cancha de tenis

radio
radio

tennis ball
pelota de tenis

ball boy
atrapapelotas

robin bird
petirrojo

window
ventana

tree
árbol

tennis player
jugador de tenis

tennis racket
raqueta de tenis

squirrel with acorn
ardilla con bellota

the museum el museo

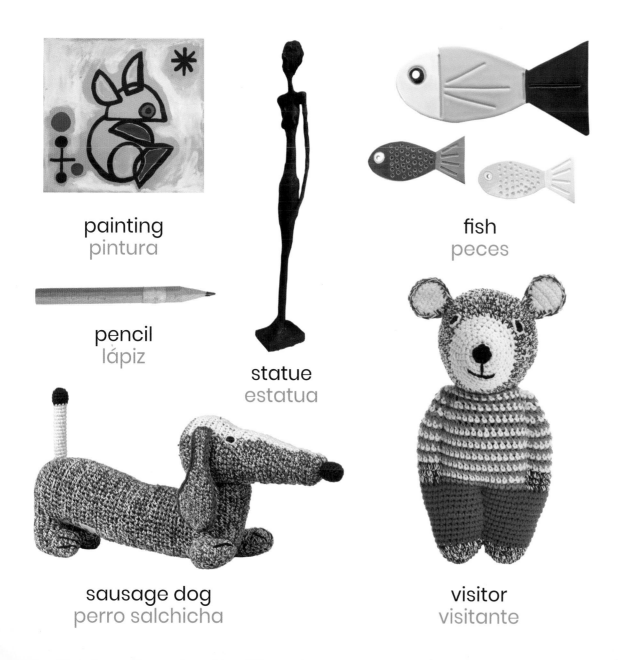

painting
pintura

pencil
lápiz

statue
estatua

fish
peces

tourists
turistas

art folder
carpeta

sausage dog
perro salchicha

visitor
visitante

camera
cámara fotográfica

the doctor el doctor

guitar
guitarra

stool
taburete

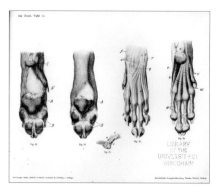

poster
cartel

patient
paciente

doctor
doctor

stethoscope
estetoscopio

handbag
bolsa

magazine
revista

toy car
carrito de juguete

the restaurant el restaurante

lobster
langosta

bottle
botella

still life
bodegón

bartender
barman

chair
silla

waiter
camarero o mesero

cake
pastel

pepper and salt
pimienta y sal

menu
menú

the gym el gimnasio

gymnast
gimnasta

basketball hoop
canasta de balocesto

sport masseur
masajista

rings
anillos

coach
entrenador

hoop and ball
aro y pelota

cones
conos

rackets
raquetas de tenis

rugby ball
balón de rugby

olympic medalist
medallista olímpico

the wedding la boda

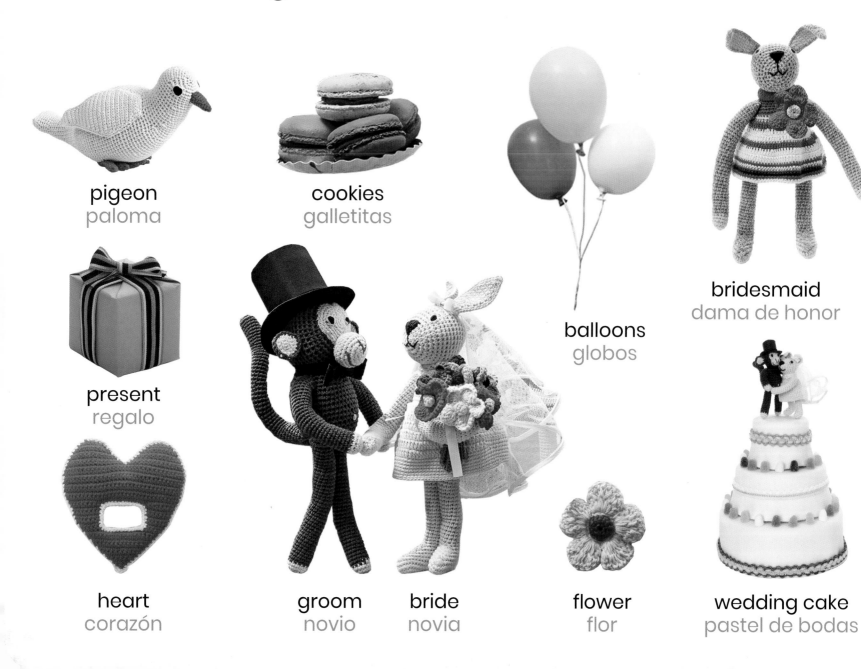

pigeon
paloma

cookies
galletitas

balloons
globos

bridesmaid
dama de honor

present
regalo

heart
corazón

groom
novio

bride
novia

flower
flor

wedding cake
pastel de bodas

the animals los animales

squirrel
ardilla

bird
pájaro

monkey
mono

mouse
ratón

bear
oso

cat
gato

pigeon
paloma

dog
perro

owl
búho

lobster
langosta

pig
cerdo

penguins
pingüinos

rabbit
conejo

fox
zorro

seafish
estrella
de mar

fish
pez

seahorse
caballito
de mar

chimp
chimpancé

human being
ser humano

stork
cigüeña

reindeer
reno

raccoon
mapache